# PANIC ATTACKS

*STOP BEING AFRAID*

*LIVE AND LOVE YOUR LIFE AGAIN*

*FIND OUT ABOUT GEORGE*

**By**

**Alan Branch**

# Contents

# Prelude (What to Expect?)

If you are looking at this book, you are looking for a way out of panic attacks, apprehension and poor experience of life. I did it for forty-plus years until one day, after many attempts, I found the answer—a simple man's answer.

As is the case in many ways, the solution lies in just looking at the problem from another angle. It could be that the answer is one that has been offered by many well-meaning people.

Sadly, they have made the case in thousands of words to maybe justify a large book, and the answer has disappeared into paper and ink! I was surprised by the ease with which I stopped the attacks.

# Introduction

To start things off, let me share the very first time I had a panic attack. As I recall, my first attack was right out of the blue, as these things often are. Because of the shock, the experience doesn't give you a chance to think about it or try and figure out what is happening to you.

I had gone to Lytham St Anne for a course on a piece of equipment, and it meant that I had to go by train from Brighton. This had to be an eight-hour trip, at the very least. Looking back, I didn't want to go as I hadn't been married long, and as is often the case, married bliss was far from a given.

The last thing I wanted to do was go some 250 miles from home. The course was fine, and the group got on. We had the usual drinks and headed for the last day. I felt fine. I was going home.

At the final chat, we sat around and talked about how good the course had been. The chief instructor stuck his hand around the door and said, "I will give diplomas to everyone because each and every one of you is the best"!

How or what happened, I do not know. All of a sudden, I was filled with a terrible fear. My throat tightened up. My heart started pounding, and I was filled with a terrible foreboding. What on earth had just happened?

I felt that I was going to pass out. If I did, I knew that an ambulance would have been called and my urgent trip home would have been cancelled. I also knew that I just had to get out of that classroom and start my journey home, but how was I going to do it? God only knew!

The first part of the journey included about three stops in London. The attack had only happened about four hours earlier, and I had no idea whether it was the beginning of a series of attacks or just a one-off.

It was an hour's trip crossing London on the underground. WOW! To be honest, the trip comes back to me even now after so many years.

In my mind, I had to be afraid of something, but what? I managed to get back home and spent the next few weeks dreading another attack. Where would it happen? How would I cope? It was pretty clear that a horrible time was coming for me.

Most of the next few weeks were spent wondering what had happened and what was the reason. The trouble was that I couldn't put a name to it. I think that this was the main difficulty in coming to terms with it.

Another lethal attack didn't happen. However, a low level of apprehension was always there. In situations like that in the past, I had always just accepted them. I viewed them with suspicion in case they bought on another attack. People I have talked to in a similar situation have agreed that my reactions were actually the same as theirs.

By that, I mean we viewed it as a mental problem, and how do you simply massage that away or understand it?

At that time, I never had this type of attack before. I had just spent four years in the Royal Air Force and had many close friends, and this had never happened before. The trouble, of course, was that there did not seem to be any reason for it. THAT IS THE WORRY THAT STAYS WITH US. THE POSSIBILITY THAT IT COULD HAPPEN AT ANY TIME!

I found out that I experienced the same heightened feelings in certain situations. Not the full onslaught, but most of the time, just a heightened state of apprehension. This is the main reason why we all keep the same level of fear going.

Taking the train or underground really got to me. I would do all sorts of things to avoid getting into these situations. How could I sit on a train with a heightened sense of apprehension, waiting for another attack?

Mostly, it didn't happen, but my life was far from happy. You cannot go through life in fear. You just don't get anywhere. Better jobs, self-confidence and self-esteem were all affected. I just couldn't figure out what it was. I always wondered if an attack could happen at any time. My brain seemed to have been taken over completely by this fear, and I couldn't see anything but the need to avoid any situation that I didn't have control over.

Of course, that is what happens to everyone that is struck with this affliction. Complete confusion and the fear you are going to pass out are merely the extent of this feeling. And before long, the feeling gradually subsides. I felt this "diminishing" feeling whenever I was attacked by this thing. It seemed to have a limited time to act.

Maybe your body gets tired, and the feeling just loses strength. I didn't realise that this apprehension would stay with me for over 50 years at varying levels.

Most of the time, there would be a feeling of awareness. An awareness that, as there wasn't a reason for it to happen in the first place, there was no stopping it from happening again at any moment.

It was such a powerful attack that the memory of it

seemed as fresh as if it had just occurred. I found out that in the future, when you have one of these attacks, you are able to keep apparently calm while inside you want to hide somewhere or just get out of the place you are in!

I look back at that time and wish I could have spent more time investigating what exactly it was that was getting to me. If I had looked further, I would have seen that the condition was far from being in the minority. In fact, it was just the opposite(Google figures of 600,000,000 worldwide).

You are a part of a huge number of people who all have the same experience because it came without warning!

The main thought that I had was when will it happen again in the future. And frankly, this is what scares you the most and alters your entire outlook on life.

This feeling, I found, has no respect for sex, age or a person's lifestyle. The real question is:"How do you cope with it"?

I think that I took the path of all or many of the other people who suffer from this phobia or anxiety/panic attacks or whatever you like to call them. I started to look at my actions, which could possibly trigger an attack. It started to take control of my life.

Deep down, I knew this, and I am sad to say there was a diminishing of self-respect that came with it. This, unfortunately, in a way, exacerbated the thought that I could experience anxiety at any time. The need to get on with your life, jobs, marriage, kids, etc., had to be coped with, and the saying "a brave man dies but once, but a coward dies a thousand times" passed through my mind on many occasions. However, when I realised what was happening, the saying couldn't have been further from the truth!

Let me also mention that visits to the dentist were a main fear. From the moment you were sitting in the waiting room and being given the call, it was awful. This is, I think, a normal reaction for people as very few people treat the dentist visit as a means of celebration.

The ones who have experienced a panic attack are actually more aware of the situation. Committed to sitting in a chair having either a filling, an extraction, or even a check-up. It didn't matter!

The fact you were committed to staying there for 20 minutes or so with the thought that the feeling could hit at any time with feelings of faintness or the terrible need to get out of the chair and just run. In the end, the result of this was easy.

Avoid the dentist at any cost, and don't risk an attack, even at the expense of the health of your teeth. I was taking the worst possible action. AVOIDANCE. That is what I was doing! Such is the power of this attack; you never seem to have the time to really get it or understand it. The apparently easiest path is to avoid it and just cope with things. Simple. Or so I thought. But in reality, it was the absolute opposite of what I should have done.

# Chapter 1: Using the Motorway

The attack only happened once, and it was on a very busy motorway. I was faced with a fairly long holdup due to the heavy volume of traffic that was on the road that day. I could see the traffic slowing, and as usual, cars and lorries were beginning to bunch up, and the feeling hit me again with frightening effect.

I could not go back or turn it off. I couldn't get out as that would have made the situation worse. These feelings were coming to me a couple of minutes after it first hit.

On a rather amusing note, I felt that I would like to get into the back of the van and hide under a tarpaulin. I wondered what would have been the reaction of the emergency services if they had come across a seventeen-stone man in this position holding up about ten miles of traffic.

I had the feeling that everyone was aware of me and my van, and I swore to myself that I would avoid this situation in future if I could. I would use minor roads in future even if it took twice the time! I didn't care. I just didn't want to have that experience again.

At that time, it didn't occur to me that I was letting

the fear control my life. Remember, these deep thoughts are not important. AVOIDANCE AGAIN!

# Chapter 2: Tube Train Journeys

Using a train that would use a tunnel was also especially worrying, so what do you do? The thought of using the tube was enough to make me feel physically sick. You alter your life to avoid these events.

Catching a bus to avoid the tunnel and then boarding the train was one of the ways I liked. It sounds stupid now, but I was into survival! Traffic journeys that meant having to use the motorway were especially a problem.

To avoid the use of an underground train, I would get to London by either walking or catching a bus because it stops every five minutes and you can get off whenever you want. All of these tricks I used to get by, but I was very aware that it was really beginning to control my life. I tried to read up about it from various books, but they were so deep that I couldn't understand a word of them.

It was pretty obvious to me that most of the writers hadn't experienced what I was experiencing and didn't give me any help at all. I am probably not being fair to these writers as I realise now when I have sorted out my demons, that they maybe did have the answer, but it was written in such a way that I just couldn't grasp it. I began to think that this thing was going to be with me forever. The trouble was, I just didn't know what it actually was: anxiety, claustrophobia, agoraphobia, or a combination of all of them.

What actually starts it off and why? I went around in circles in those days until I could stand it no more and did the thing I should have done earlier and reported sick. I made an appointment at the local hospital that I knew cared for people who suffered from mental problems.

It wasn't easy. I entered the office of a senior nurse and hoped with all my heart that I didn't know him.

We had a long talk, and I emptied my mind of all that had happened to me up to that point. He was very sympathetic, of course, but said, "To be frank, in my experience, which is extensive, you look completely at ease. You look like the last person I would have figured to suffer from extreme anxiety. But I am well aware that this is a genuine issue for you. Let me see what can be done".

He gave me a handful of typewritten advice that he felt would help to explain what it was and how to cope with it. He also gave me very good advice, which I did find of some use. He advised me to give up cigarettes and coffee. This advice did help in that I definitely felt better. As an afterthought, there is no doubt in my mind that there is much more advice available now, with more and more people ready to talk about anxiety.

However, the papers he gave me didn't remove the anxiety. The advice to take big breaths and see all the good things in my life just didn't do it. I still had to analyse future events and evaluate the potential threat. The book *Do The Thing You Are Frightened of And The Fear Will Go Away* didn't work at all. I just had to go through the same old manipulation for every event as before. I think the word SURVIVED best describes how I lived back in those tumultuous days. I think I was also poisoning myself with bags of homoeopathic remedies that tasted like God knows what, but all they did was make me spend more time on the toilet.

I would like to say that with age came enlightenment, but sadly, it didn't happen for me. I became very cynical when I tried to find out what was wrong with me. I couldn't believe some of the rubbish I read. I still had no idea why the feelings would come to me. I just couldn't put a name on it. I was resigned to go through the rest of my life battling, if it isn't too strong a word, to get by. I also thought with the decline of self-respect came a sense of underachievement.

Please do not think that I was sorry for myself! I had got to the ripe old age of 79 and survived. I had enjoyed a long and happy marriage, children, grandchildren and even one great-granddaughter. I seemed to get a feeling that I had survived and kept going, but oh dear, if only I could get to the bottom of it and start to enjoy life more.

Looking back then, there seemed to be an answer there somehow, but it all seemed to be a mental problem, and how the blazes can anyone do anything about that sort of complaint after all.

The trouble is, if you don't know what is happening to you, you can't begin to put it right. All you can do is react to it and suffer. I had shown some courage and kept going on when all seemed to be pretty dreadful. During this time, the thought that the answer may be near gave me hope. But what was the answer!?

What started it? What brought it on? Until I could understand that, I knew I couldn't beat it. At that time, I felt that I was suffering from some mental aberration, and you can't just rub that away. I suppose you can start hitting the bottle or living on drugs that are now readily available, but, as is usual, there is a price to pay for that!

# Chapter 3: Holidays Abroad

Around that time, I was put in a position in which I had to take a plane trip for a two-week holiday abroad. Up to that point, I always got out of this situation by pompously telling my family that we hadn't seen all of our own country and we should leave foreign trips until we had exhausted the UK. I reckon I could have kept that up for years, but both our kids were in their late teens, and they were the only people amongst their friends who had never been abroad!

I knew that I was faced with the biggest trial yet. For weeks before the holiday date, I went through the process of getting on a train, heading to the airport and then booking in. All the time, getting closer to the steel tube coffin that I was going to have to sit in and pretend I was looking forward to it.

Then, sitting down and the stewardess slamming the door shut like the clap of doom and oh my God, what next!!! I went to see my doctor and told him I had a terrible fear of flying, and he gave me a couple of pills for both outward and incoming flights. They worked. But now, along with all other escapes, I was using drugs. This trip, however, would make up for all the other times I had avoided flying.

Some years later, I agreed to go on a trip with two friends, which would be a four-hour trip. I thought I could cope with this by going to my doctor and getting two more pills. Sadly, my old doctor had retired, and the new one refused to give me any drugs for the trip. What a mess! It was at this time I decided to go back to my books and find out what it was all about.

Over the years, while studying books on various suggestions by the authors, I discovered that some were medically trained, and some were living in a different universe. They just didn't get it.

Somewhere in the dim and distant past, I had read that one should let the feelings go through you. I remembered that I had tried it and felt that how do you let these feelings do that? They were stuck in my stomach, lungs and head. Where on earth could I let them go?

Also, what was I letting go of!? There was another word in a particular book that said ACCEPTANCE, and at long last, the word began to have some meaning.

I also had read an eminent doctor who suggested that the adrenal gland, in some cases, becomes over-sensitised. MY GOD, it felt like somebody had just walked into a semi-dark room and switched the light on. The whole thing made sense to me. Why couldn't I try and ACCEPT that the feelings I was experiencing were **PHYSICAL** ones and were being generated by an over-sensitised adrenalin gland determined to pump me full of adrenalin for no apparent reason? I hadn't got claustrophobia or a brain tumour or was slowly going mad.

Obviously, if you were put into a position of terror, you would welcome the adrenalin gland giving you an extra 10 miles per hour speed to get you to safety. Perfectly reasonable. But what if you were in Boots the chemist and leaned down to pick up a tube of toothpaste, and George kicks in? I kid you not. It happened. After that, it was difficult to visit Boots after that.

# Chapter 4: Flying

I vividly remember a holiday with my wife to Benalmadena. I went through the usual gut-wrenching feelings up to the flight. I took buckets of herbal things, and whereas it didn't stop the feelings of expecting the "rush", it didn't actually happen. I got off the plane pretty happy with myself.

Sadly, all through the holiday, the apprehension of the return trip was never far away. Before long came the return trip, and the plane was totally full. I was not sitting next to my wife, but I thought since I had completed one-half of the trip, I was going to be OK.

Eventually, we took off, and I tried to sit quietly and relax. I happened to look up, and it was one of those planes that had a screen up front that showed you how far you had gone and how long you had left. The attack hit me like a train! The main feeling was that I was having a heart attack or just about to have one. I found myself staring at the screen. Being sick all over the guy next to me or just fainting were the feelings in my mind.

All the time that blasted screen looked like it had stopped. I could take it no more and reached out to grab the steward, and I missed him. I was actually going to tell him I was having a heart attack.

At that moment, I felt a slight decline of the feeling, and during the rest of the flight, it gradually went away. I think the body just can't keep those feelings going. Either the body gets tired, or the adrenal gland loses strength. I got back to Gatwick and promised myself I would find a cure for myself at all costs and never dread journeys again in whatever vehicle I was in.

My mind went back to the doctor who had suggested that these attacks could be the result of an over-sensitised adrenal gland. This suggestion made sense to me. Why couldn't I try and accept that the feelings I felt were PHYSICAL ones and were being generated by this gland, which was in a state of over sensitivity? I felt that I now had an actual opponent to face, and I could give him a physical presence. I decided to give him a name, and I decided on GEORGE.

If I could accept the feeling as a purely physical experience, I could treat him like any other physical pain and just accept it. I began to look forward to accepting George, not facing it. I started to venture into those situations that, in the past, had caused me so much grief. I would say to myself, *Come on, George, do your worst!*

*Come and sit with me on this plane, train, bus or car.*

I knew that if George started to appear, it was just a little gland having a spasm. I just didn't care. I had lost my fear of him. He never appeared again! I would also like to say, especially with men, it is expected that you act strong and appear rock solid in front of your family.

I think that they saw me in this way anyway. I think if you are afflicted with this horrible thing and that you carry on anyway as best you can, you should be proud. You have been tested and found the courage to do your best. It is easy to go through life without a test like this. Be proud of yourself even when things may start coming at you. Call for George! Don't worry. Like him and accept him.

Don't be surprised if you never hear from him again. I am now 81 years of age, and the feeling of freedom is totally thrilling. You do not have to psych yourself up every time you go out of your comfort zone. Take your George with you. I also found that the low level of trepidation left me as I felt that George's strength was always with me.

My life, even at my age, started to get better, and so will yours! The powerful feeling of self-confidence grew and grew. One thing I will repeat is my suggestion of giving up smoking and caffeine. It certainly helps the feeling of feeling healthier. It helps in giving you the realisation that you lose the fear of that thing, and the result is that it disappears. I am a normal 81-year-old and do not give in to fanciful thoughts. I have lived a fairly varied existence and am a lot more experienced than when I was 20.

There is an awful lot of publicity about this complaint nowadays. Many public figures suffer from it and, thankfully, are not afraid to publicise it. As I said, it has no regard for sex, class, or age. It is almost comforting to know that some medical professionals suffer from it. But finding GEORGE has worked for me. Getting into lifts, trains, planes meetings and motorway journeys.

In fact, 101 different ways of feeling overwhelmed have disappeared. TAKE GEORGE WITH YOU.HE IS A TOWER OF STRENGTH.I call it George. You pick your own name!

Remember, you can take strength from what you have been through. If you look around, how many people you see are going to experience for the first time the dreadful feelings when the panic/anxiety attacks start? You have survived and shown great fortitude and courage. Attributes you didn't realise you had. Be proud and go forward with your life and ambitions. Don't forget to take George with you.

# Chapter 5: How My Journey Began

Back in2019,after some 40 years of coping, if that is the right word, with panic attacks, I decided to try and sort out my problem once and for all. I had tried much of the recognised advice from books and videotapes and a visit to a hospital that apparently "specialised" in this sort of thing, but to no avail.

To achieve this, I decided to write a book. It was called *A Simple Man's Guide to Stop Panic Attacks, Call it George.* This may seem an odd title, but if you read the book, you will understand why!

Writing the book and actually bearing my soul, so to speak, seemed to remove all embarrassment and shame. If you like, it allowed me to escape the bullying of this wretched condition that apparently afflicts some half a billion people worldwide (we are not alone).

The result of writing this book had a remarkable effect on me. It seemed that as I wrote the book, the fear of this ailment seemed to diminish. I think the actual fact of bearing my soul and sharing my pain was cathartic. I felt a growing feeling of peace as I wrote my book until the very end. I sat back and felt an almost overwhelming peace that hadn't been in my life since my teens.

Sitting and revelling in this, I couldn't believe that I had actually found a way that I could stop these attacks. It seemed too easy, and I didn't conform to any of the books that I had read on the subject, and let me tell you, there were many!

As I mentioned earlier, maybe they were too deep in their analysis and mostly seemed to dwell on why they happened, and I found the mystics of trying to figure out what my brain was doing was way beyond my pay grade.

It was far easier to start coping with the physical effects of these attacks. This is why I decided to call it George— "IT" being my adrenal gland.

When I realised that I could identify the reaction to an over-sensitised gland, I was overwhelmed. Giving it a name called George helped. Feel free to call your adrenal gland whatever you like! Having a name gave it a physical presence similar to a bad toothache, a gastric attack, a bad muscle strain or whatever you like.

I knew for a fact that if George appeared, I was confident that I could accept it for what it was: an over-sensitised adrenal gland having a great time blasting adrenalin to all my organs and frightening the daylights out of us. I would immediately say to myself, "Welcome,

George", and make myself carry on doing whatever I wanted to do.

Obviously, I felt that this couldn't be that easy! I carried on with my life, awaiting another visitation. As time went by, do you know what? It didn't reappear!! I began to lose my fear of it, and that feeling grew stronger as time went by until the time came (fairly quickly) when I didn't think of it at all. I had completely lost my fear of it.

I feel sad that I hadn't worked this out much earlier in my life. Maybe my age has given me the wisdom to see GEORGE for what it was. Being plagued by this awful complaint has changed my life, and I regret that I didn't realise my potential.

However, I am blessed with a truly wonderful family and set of friends, so it hasn't been a complete loss. Maybe having to cope with GEORGE has given me the character and personality that has given me the blessings that I have. I am sure that if you are reading this, please don't feel depressed or downhearted. Coping with these attacks and surviving with jobs, schools, relationships, partnerships, or any of a dozen other situations is making you stronger, and I am positive a better person. After all, you have been tested, and you are living with it. Think of all the people who have yet to experience it.

In the four years since writing the book and being free from "GEORGE", I have endeavoured to build myself up after all those years of being battered by George. It was like building a protective wall about myself. They were small steps and easily attained, and everyone rebuilt my self-esteem, which, over the years, has taken many knocks.

# Chapter 6: Dancing

This may not appeal to everybody. And frankly, it didn't appeal to me as I had always raced for the bar when the music started as usual, wondering when GEORGE was going to pay a visit. I had always felt that I would like to be able to dance, especially as my wife always fancied it.

Anyway, I decided to give it a go and see how it went. I chose modern jive, and it turned out to be incredible. Within weeks, I was reasonably competent, but more importantly, my self-esteem went up by leaps and bounds. FIRST ON THE FLOOR!

I followed this up by increasing my exposure to situations that, in the past, had caused problems, and in every case, I won. It is incredible what confidence that does for your personal strength. It doesn't seem to matter what standard your dance capabilities are. I think that dancing means you are in close personal contact with other human beings who generate the warmth that builds one's confidence.

Once you see George for what it truly is and you get your life back, try and concentrate on building your self-esteem because this lack of self-esteem will continue to cause you problems.

Try and find an aspect of your life that, deep down, however minor, it seems that you feel could improve your life. It could be as small as changing a hairstyle that you have always wanted to do; I have found that taking these small steps has helped me enormously.

Another step I took, which I can't praise enough, is the importance of taking good vitamins. The result of this step was a very gradual improvement in my health to the extent I have never felt better.

All this, the book, the acknowledgement of George, and the steps to build up my lost esteem have made me realise that sometimes it is good to take a sideways step in looking at a problem and in recognition of GEORGE. There's no doubt the physical effects of an overactive adrenal gland are awful, and trying to figure out what was going on in one's head is impossible for a sufferer to understand.

After all, if 1001 technical people writing books can only potentially suggest a reason for the mental aberrations based on so many theories and not offer a sound, sensible cure (I do not suggest that drugs are the answer). Then, it is far better to see it from a physical angle.

I say, look at the physical pain that is so obvious

and treat it as such. So many sufferers, I am sure, are otherwise healthy, sound people of both sexes and of varying ages trying to cope with the effects of George. They are unable to go forward in life. What a terrible waste! Take George with you. I think you will find that he is hardly any problem at all and you will lose all fear of him and start to reach your real potential.

# Conclusion

When I decided to write my book *A Simple Man's Guide For Stopping Panic Attacks*, I decided on a simple way to accept the physical manifestation of panic attacks. Also, I gave it a physical presence, which I called George.

I needed to give George a place in my life that I could recognise and accept as a benign event and not one that was to be feared and dreaded if he arrived. Hence, the adrenal gland became George. I decided also to carry around with me a token that made me accept George as a normal occurrence and not one to be feared.

In doing this, the attacks stopped, and more importantly, the apprehension left me. As you are aware, the apprehension of a panic attack is as bad if not worse than the actual event!!!

The apprehension I found made me change my ways in what I did, my ambitions, relationships and because of the fear of what could arrive out of the blue. The actual attacks when they came, horrible though they were, only stayed for a while and then disappeared.

## Self-Esteem

The building of self-esteem is vital after one is relieved of the attacks. Many years of erosion of confidence took its toll. As a result, the rebuilding of confidence/self-esteem is imperative. I found the George plaque very helpful as a reminder that George isn't that big a deal.

The George plaque reminds me of what I have achieved and how the plaque is no longer anything to be frightened of. Maybe I have been lucky in the total removal of the attacks. I don't think so. Giving George a physical presence immediately stopped the attacks.

This happened because I had to cope with the unknown (in my head) and see George as a bully who could be accepted. And you know what happens once you do this: you lose your fear of the bully! You are a bigger person if you do.

Before you know it, you are making friends with every bad thing in your life and boy, oh boy, it builds your mental/physical strength. People, places, and situations are all accepted as never before. Want a better job? You can go for it. Fly to Spain? It's no more challenging than a two-hour car journey. People? They are all a mirror image.

In other words, you gain an advantage by going

through hell. You are a person who has seen it all and completely transformed yourself. **REMEMBER GEORGE!**

At this point in my life, I can thankfully claim that I no longer have any fear of George, and the George plaque in my pocket has become nothing more than a familiar piece. Later on, it reminded me that my adrenal gland (George) had become over-sensitised and liable to give me a jolt out of the blue.

Similarly, I thought having a bad knee that every now and again would remind me of a wonky patella. Having lost the fear of an attack opened up everything for me. I think that the fear or apprehension of an attack keeps the complaint going long after it should.

Once I lost the fear of it, my life changed, sadly, long after it should have. Before George, it was like being in chains and aiding and abetting that awful feeling of loss of self-esteem. It is extremely hard to grow into your full potential with the dead weight of George hanging on to you and influencing every decision you make.

So, why treat George as an enemy instead of accepting it as a character-forming aid for oneself? It can enable you to move forward and become a stronger, more confident person. At least, that has been the case for me, and I know you will also have the same extraordinary results. Bless you all!